Dawn of a New Day

From Chains to Freedom

A Collection of Inspirational Poems
by *Alba McCarthy*

Creative Force Press

Creative Force Press

Dawn of a New Day
© 2014 by Alba McCarthy

This title is also available as an eBook. Visit
www.CreativeForcePress.com/titles for more information.

Published by Creative Force Press
4704 Pacific Ave, Suite C, Lacey, WA 98503
www.CreativeForcePress.com

Scriptures quoted in this book are taken from the King James Version.

ISBN: 978-1-939989-09-3

Author photo: © Photographer Gina Esposito 2014 | www.ginaesposito.com
Printed in the United States of America

Dedication

This book is dedicated to my children, James, Stephen and Crystal Rose, my daughters-in-love, Robin and Cristina and my beautiful granddaughters Chloe Rae and Mackenzie Rose. Thank you for your love and support and all the joy you have brought into my life. I am so proud to call you mine. God has truly blessed me. My prayer for you is that you will be strong in the Lord and in the power of His might and do all for the Glory of God! I know God has a great plan for each one of you.

In loving memory of my beloved mother, Gloria Argentina, who raised 17 children and made it look easy. Her faith in God was unshakeable and she lived a life of love, always doing for others. Her quiet presence spoke volumes to those around her giving them comfort and strength. And to my sister Linda, you left us far too soon. You are both greatly missed and are forever in my heart.

If the son therefore shall make you free, ye shall be free indeed.

John 8:36

Table of Contents

Introduction

Each one of us faces challenges and difficult life situations we have to navigate through. I am no different than anyone else. I have had my share of valleys in my life. Some valley experiences felt like they would never end. Some of the trials we go through are the result of bad choices, some out of ignorance, and some out of rebellion. But whatever the case may be, they are still difficult, and I dare to say impossible, to overcome without God.

The poems I have written were penned as I found my way to the mountain top. Many times, while going through very difficult challenges, I despaired of going on and just wished the world would stop so I could get off! It was during some of these low points in my life that I began to write. Many of these poems express the cry of my heart. God knows our hurts, our pain and the deepest longing of our soul. I am so grateful that during these times He was always with me and never left me alone. At times I didn't know He was there and I couldn't feel Him, but when I look back, I know He was there all the time. Not only was He there, but He surrounded me with amazing people along the way. They were there to pray for me, encourage me and challenge me to a deeper faith. They are the angels in my life. To these special people I would like to say thank you. Only eternity will tell the difference you have made in my life.

Going through these times has taught me many valuable lessons, which I am now able to share with others and encourage them on to greater faith and hope for tomorrow. I pray that these poems will speak to those places in your life as you navigate through some of your own challenges, and that you will find your way to the mountain top and be able to say, "The best is yet to come!"

Blessings,
Alba

Sitting outside on the deck of my home on the 4th of July some years ago, these words came pouring out of my heart. On a day which celebrates freedom for our country, what a revelation to find that true freedom is in Christ alone through His sacrifice on the cross. Amazing Love!

Chains

What are these chains that hold me so tightly? I cannot see their circle around me, but I can feel their deathlike grip. What is their power that they can choke the life from me, rendering me weak and powerless?
Its hold is so tight that the capability to move is no longer possible.

Who holds the chains? How do I get free?
What are these chains made of?
I take a closer look. I see each link bound together holding one another in its own circle giving the chain its power.

I see a link of **Pride**, strong and haughty.
I see a link of **Selfishness**, wanting its own way.
I see a link of **Vanity**, hoping to gain attention.
I see a link of **Lust**, wanting what is impure.
There is a circle of **Jealousy**, wanting what is someone else's.
The link of **Dishonesty**, struggling to hide the truth.
The truth cannot be hidden.
There alongside is a link of **Self-Righteousness**,
Thinking it is better and stronger than the next link.

I examine the links to find the secret of this chain.
Which is the strongest? I cannot tell?

I stop, I pray, I ask for wisdom and understanding.
As I open my eyes, I see it - the secret revealed.
The chain is a chain of sin. Each link unique and separate

Yet working so effectively together.
Its power made stronger by each little link
Making its vise-like grip undeniable.

Will I remain in its grip forever? Will I willingly submit
To the bondage that strangles me?

I keep seeking and praying for the freedom I long for.
As I pray, I see it - I see a hand. I look closer.
The hand is scarred, as though it were pierced.
I look closer still - I see a cross. The answer becomes clear.
At the foot of the cross I see what was once a chain
Broken to bits, rendered useless. Each link powerless.

I find the answer I have been searching for.
*In place of Pride, I find **Humility** - He gave His life.*
*Selfishness can no longer take - **Selflessness** now takes its place.*
*Vanity: no longer vain, but **boasting in another** and the work*
He has done.

*Lust, now only **wants more of His Love**.*
*Jealousy; now replaced with **Giving**, until it can give no more.*
*Dishonesty; now overshadowed by the **Truth of the Cross**.*
*Self-righteousness now stands in **His Righteousness**.*

The chain has lost its power. Sin has been dealt a deadly blow.
The chain has been broken.

I have been set free by the power of the Cross!

John 8:36

14

Unanswered questions are never easy. They bring frustration, anxiety, and can paralyze us from moving forward. As I wrestled with many unanswered questions in my own life, I was prompted to put pen to paper and this poem was the result. Only now can I see that He truly did have all the answers, and only through seeking God did I come to find His answers for myself. He healed my emotions and taught me to overcome. My emotions now serve me, not master me. God has the power to answer your questions so that you too will be an overcomer.

Questions

How? When? Where? Why?
How did I get to this place?
When did I lose control?
Where did these feelings come from?
Why am I in this turmoil?

God, only You know.
When I have no answers,
I know You have all the answers.

Tell me what I need to know.
Why do I feel the way I do?
How do I get free from the emotions that control me?
Where is the courage I need to go on?
When will I overcome?

Psalm 13:1-2

On a warm summer day, feeling a bit down and just wanting to get away, I decided to take a ride down by the water. I wanted to just sit and enjoy the beauty and serenity that I always find at the beach. As I was leaving the house, I heard a still small voice telling me to take pen and paper along. Surprised by the command, I did so, and this poem was the result of that obedience.

Dear God

Where do I go when the storms of life
Rage around me? Who will shelter me?
When I feel abandoned with no one to care,
Where do I go?
When I have been tested and tried and
Feel like a failure, who will have me?
When I feel alone and unloved,
Who will love me?
When the hurt goes so deep that I cannot
Stand the pain any longer, who will care?
When temptation haunts me and I am weak
And about to give in, who will rescue me?
Oh God, I have only you. There is no one else.
You are my rescue, my hiding place.
Shelter me under the wings of the Almighty.
Lead me beside the still waters so that I
Might be silent and feel Your leading.
When I struggle, may I come to the place
Where I realize I am never alone. You are
Always there, loving me, waiting for me to
Trust and let go of all my fears and failures,
Bringing me to a place of complete freedom.
May I find that place of rest where I realize
You know what's best for me. Trusting that
Your ways are higher than my ways,
Knowing that You do all things well.
Lord help me to live in the complete freedom

That You have so lovingly given to me.

AMEN

Psalm 22:24

I have found that the hardest part of praying is waiting for the answers to come. It is difficult to wait expectantly with hope and faith when our flesh is screaming in opposition with doubt, fear and unbelief flooding in. Unfortunately, waiting is necessary and is just a built-in part of the process.

As I was in this process, these words came to me. I pray they will encourage you to be patient and still.

As I Wait

Lord, I wait for You, knowing you have heard the cry of my heart.
Lord, I wait for You, knowing you have the answers that I need.
Lord, I wait for You, knowing I need to be patient and still.
Lord, I wait for You, refusing to respond in fear.
Lord, I wait for You, knowing you are the Good Shepherd
Who takes care of His sheep.
Lord, I wait for You, knowing You are able to work,
Even through my inability.
Lord, I wait for You, knowing You are faithful, even though
I am sometimes unfaithful to You.
Lord, I wait for You, knowing that as I am waiting,
You are working, working on me, changing me,
That I may be a vessel of honor, so that You may be glorified.

Lord, let Your glory be revealed in my life,
As I Wait.

Psalm 40:1

Why Worry
When You
Can Pray?

Worry

Let go of the worry
The battle is His
The answer is on the way

Let go of doubt and unbelief
For this will make you stray

He's heard your prayers
He'll answer you
Of this, you can be sure
Although, the answer may not be
The one you're hoping for

Remember, He has your best in mind
Be sure that this is true
He'll help you through 'til the journey ends
Sometimes, He'll carry you

So, do not worry, do not fret
His love will see you through
Walk in faith and do not doubt
He is your closest friend!

Matthew 6:25-34

No one likes to be alone - at least not for any great length of time. Even the scriptures tell us that it is not good for man to be alone. (Genesis 2:18) Ecclesiastes 4:9 says, "Two are better than one." But, sometimes aloneness is necessary. Often, it is in the solitary place that we find God. It is in that place alone that we can know we are never alone. What a comfort to know that He will never leave us nor forsake us!

A Solitary Place

Sometimes the treasures in life can only
Be found in a solitary place
Yet this is the place we fear most to be
Alone, Afraid, Vulnerable

What good can come of this lonely place?
The silence is deafening, the shadows eerie
Fear stalking at every turn

This place resembles the valley
The valley of the shadow of death
Is there a treasure to be found here?

The treasure can only be found when
I submit to the will of the Shepherd
Knowing this is the place He has chosen
For me to be right now
A place I must pass through
That I may find my way to the mountain top

The treasure can be found when in the silence
I hear the voice of the Shepherd speak to my heart saying
"Peace be still"
Or, when I look behind the shadows and
See the rainbow with the promise telling me
"I will never leave you, nor forsake you"

It is then I know I have found the treasure
There is nothing to fear
I am never alone
Only in a "solitary place"

John 14:18

As I prepared a lesson to share with the men in the jail where I minister, I was hoping to have a little story or antidote to share with them. Then I stumbled upon this poem which I had just written two weeks prior, only to find it lined up exactly with what I was planning to teach. God has a way of supplying in unusual ways.

The Journey

The journey started out so smooth, the way it seemed so bright
Somehow, although I don't know when, the light it turned to night

The darkness came in like a flood, so difficult to see
I couldn't for the life of me tell how this could ever be

As I look back on my journey its apparent I failed to see
The truth was right in front of me, but yet I didn't believe
The deception was so subtle, distracted were my eyes
Only now can I see that destruction was disguised

It took the form of pleasure, empty promises and good times
These had only lasted for a pitifully short time
The journey lost its pleasure, the road became so hard and long
Still I had no answers to this road that I was on

Further on my journey hoping to find the light of day
I remembered all the stories I had learned along the way
I heard that God did love me and sent His son to die
He shed His blood on Calvary where He was crucified

He paid the price I could not pay, my sin upon Him laid
I did not have to stay my course, I could now turn away

I chose repentance and then turned to the road that led to life
I now know love and joy and peace, and with Him am crucified

Now the path is easy and the burdens they are light
I'll journey on till the journey ends
To the place where there is no night

Revelation 22:5

The Promised Land is just that – Promised!

Our eternal life starts here and now in this life when we become born again - born of God with His nature. We can now live the life He has promised, *abundant life*, as Jesus said, "I am come that they might have life, and that they might have it more abundantly." (John 10:10)

Catch the Vision!

Visions of the Promised Land

Oh, that my eyes might see what You see
The finished product of what I can be

I'll not settle for less than what You have planned
I will finish the task that You put in my hand

So, as I press toward the mark, let me finish the race
May I finish strong, each step marked by Your Grace
May my vision be clear, my path straight and smooth
Unhindered by fear of what man can do

Let me never tire of doing my best
Knowing then that You'll do the rest

So, Good Shepherd, hold my hand

Lead me on to the PROMISED LAND

Deuteronomy 6:3

So many of us go through life living under our circumstances; buried under a load of cares. God has intended so much more for us.

Deuteronomy 28:13 tells us, "And the Lord shall make thee the head, and not the tail; and thou shalt be above only, and thou shalt not be beneath."

Let us allow Him to bring us up higher!

A Higher Place

Lift me to a higher place, a place where the chaotic circumstances
Of my life are irrelevant. A place where all that matters is
Knowing You.
Teach me to trust you above all else

Lift me to a higher place where the noise of my life crashing
Around me is silenced and all I hear is Your still small voice.
Teach me to have Faith

Lift me to a higher place where the passions of this life
Are dimmed by the embrace of Your Sweet Spirit.
Teach me to Love you more

Lift me to a higher place where my fears can no longer torment me,
A place where Your comforting presence embraces me.
Teach me of your Perfect Peace

Lift me to a higher place where my suffering is seen
In the light of what You suffered for me at Calvary.
Teach me to be an Over comer

Lift me to a higher place where the pain in my life
Is drowned by the joy that You give.
Teach me Contentment

Lift me to a higher place where the troubles of this life
Are but a stepping stone to a higher place with You.

31

Teach me to have an Eternal perspective

LORD, lift me to a higher place, a place where all I need is You!

2 Corinthians 4:16-18

Why is it so difficult to find the time to pray?

There are always interruptions, things on the 'to do' list and so many things pressing for our attention. We wonder why our lives are out of control. Yet the answer is so simple: being connected to the only One who knows what we need by prayer and supplication.

Divinely Abiding

Abiding...
Abiding in the vine
Sounds so simple
Just Abide...
Easy, restful, trusting...

Then the truth of life knocks loudly at the door
There's no time to squander...no time to rest

Life is in turmoil
So much to be done...
Things need attention
Must get on the run...

Abiding now turns to a brief prayer whispered in haste
Don't have the time to pray...then WAIT?!

It sounds like a great idea LORD
I'd love to sometime
But, right now I'm busy...just don't have the time
Commitments to tend to, there's work to be done
Problems need solving and I've just begun

Lord, Help Me! I'm weary...I've no strength to go on
My life is in chaos, all peace is gone

What is the answer to this misery of mine?

Gently You whisper...

ABIDE IN THE VINE!

John 15:5

The greatest miracle the world will ever see is a changed heart.

Sinful man transformed into the image of the Creator!

34

Creator of Miracles

You are a God who brings beauty from ashes
You are a God who creates something from nothing
You are a God who brings life where there was death
You are a God who brings peace where there once was fear
You are a God who brings joy from sadness
You are a God who brings love where there once was hate
You alone are the Creator of miracles
Only You can change the heart of man

Create in me a clean heart, O God, that others may see a miracle in
me.

Psalm 51:10

Busyness is the thief of the soul. Oh, to be still and to be in the presence of the Maker of the universe! Our hearts long to be there, yet our soulish ways battle against it. The spirit man and our flesh are at war.

"The Kingdom of heaven suffereth violence, and the violent take it by force." (Matthew 11:12)

Let's fight to live in His presence!

In the Stillness of Your Presence

In the stillness of Your presence is where life begins

This is the place where rivers of living water begin
To overflow and sooth my soul

A place where the cares of this world are defeated
By the remembrance of who You are

The thought of You causes faith to arise
And I can soar like an eagle

It is at this place, high above the distresses of life
Where I can see Your sovereign hand and all You brought to pass

Let me keep my perspective, my eyes on the cross
Remembering all You gave and what it cost

Now, when the cares of life start closing in
I'll run to the place where all must begin

A place where confusion no longer exists
A place where fear fades into peace
A place where death and life now meet
Let me live my life

IN THE STILLNESS OF YOUR PRESENCE!

Psalm 16:11

This is a word from the Father to His children. He longs for you to know how much He loves you and that He only desires the best for you.

My Children

My children, see the raindrops?
I formed these to remind you that I see your every tear.

My children, feel the wind blow?
I created the wind so that you may know the freedom I have for
you in Me.

My children, see the snow?
I made it so that in its whiteness you would be reminded of My
purity and how you could be changed to be more like Me.

My children, see the flames of fire?
I set the fire so that you would know of My burning passion and
the passion I desire for you to have for Me.

My children, see the springs of water?
This I have given as a sign to you that I am the Living Water that
refreshes you.

My children, see the trees, their branches laden with much fruit?
This is My desire for you, to bear much fruit for Me as you allow
My Spirit to be manifested in and through you.

My children, see the flowers?
I created them in all their splendor that you may know that I will
dress you in robes of righteousness.

My children, see the birds of the air?
I have used them to show you that I am well able to provide for
your every need, just as I care for the sparrow.

My children, see the fields of grain?
I have put them there so that you would know that I will sustain
you with food for your spirit, as well as your body.

My children, see my Word?
I have left it as a love letter to let you know just how much
I Love You!

My children, see the blood?
I have shed it so that you would have a way to Me.

Come, My children, come and live!

Galatians 5:1

His ways are so much higher than our ways. I think majestic is a good fit; a proper word to describe them. He never ceases to amaze us with His extraordinary surprises. He is worthy of our service and our love!

Your Majestic Ways

The majesty of Your ways cause me to
Stand in awe as I see Your plan unfold
Though I cannot pretend to understand
When through these trials I go
When I feel the pressure and feel the squeeze
It's at this time I must bow my knees
This is the place my faith must rest
Do I trust my God, or do I fail the test
The test is where my faith is tried by fire
Bringing about Your holy desire
Your desire is for me to be set free
Always putting my trust in Thee
So, let me wait without a doubt,
All for my good You'll bring about
Let my trust be strong
My love be true
May all I do be done for You

1 Peter 12-13

The *joy* of the Lord is our strength. Open yourself to the fountain He has supplied, and let the *joy* overflow and touch the lives of those around you. We are blessed to be a blessing!

Fountain of Joy

Your joy is a fountain full of deliverance
Waiting for those who'll receive
The river unending, freely flowing
For those who'll only believe

Open the floodgates
Pour out on my life all of Your blessings today
May I not hinder You by my lack of faith
Knowing I've nothing to fear

For by Your good pleasure Your joy is to give
All in abundance to me

Let me receive all your goodness untold
So to others a blessing I'll be.

John 15:11

God manifest in the flesh.

The babe in a manger, now soon coming King.

King of Kings!
Lord of Lords!

Who is this Man?

He is the righteousness of God displayed on a cross
He is Holiness unveiled for all to see
He is Purity soaked in blood
He is the Word whispering I LOVE YOU!
He is the Creator giving His life for those He created
He is Love dying for the unlovely
He is the Prince of Peace in a world full of chaos
He is the Mighty Warrior come to set the captives free
He is Majesty in a vast universe
He is Perfect in an imperfect world
He is Truth in a world full of lies
He is Forever in a world ruled by time
He is Everything before anything was
He is Hope lifting us up out of our graves
He is The One with the scars in His hands

He is the Savior ....HE IS JESUS!

Hebrews 2:10
Matthew 1:21

In our modern day, where a brief text is a highly used mode of communication, busy signals and answering machines are the norm. Is there any hope of connecting with a human voice; with someone who is there for us? Isn't it refreshing to know there is someone who wants to hear from us at any time, day or night? God longs to communicate with us and to have us tell Him about our cares and concerns. He enjoys our companionship.

Incredible!

The Prayer of the Saints

The prayer of the Saints is what God loves to hear
The sound is like incense reaching His ears

He loves to answer, He loves to give
It gives Him great pleasure to hear from His kids

So call out to Him, He desires to help
All for our good He will bring about

Call in the morning, call Him at noon
Call in the evening, He's waiting for you

His line's never busy
He's never too tired, never too moody or preoccupied

Call out today, you'll be glad that you did
He has so much to offer, so much to give

He'll give you great peace that you've never known
He'll give you great joy to call all your own

Just give Him your burdens, He'll carry them for you
It gives Him great pleasure to do this for you

Call out in the night hours, He's up anyway
He'd love to hear all about your day

1 Thessalonians 5:17

Change is inevitable. Life *is* change.

Some seasons are wonderful; we hope they never end. Some seasons are painful; we don't know how we will ever survive.

But the most important change is the change of our heart; that we would learn to love as He loves and be changed into His image. Let the seasons of our lives create a beautiful change in us

The Seasons of Life

Though the seasons of life may come and go, there is one thing
which does not change: our Father in Heaven, and His love always
remains the same.

There are seasons of sorrow, seasons of pain, and seasons of
laughter and joy.
Mountains and valleys are strewn in my path, but of this one thing
I am sure...
I am sure of the love of my Father, compassionate, merciful, kind.
His love will never leave me even till the end of time.

So, why should I worry? Why should I fear?
All things He'll use for my good.

Every season is a blessing from above
Transforming me with His love.

At the end of the seasons when my life is at an end
I pray I'll look like my Father, my Savior, and friend.

Lord, change me as I walk through the seasons of my life.

Ecclesiastes 3:1-8

Love
The inexpressible gift
The longing of every heart
To love and to be loved

God's greatest gift!

The Gift of Love

The unending gift of LOVE
Who can comprehend it
A place of safety
Always secure

Fear does not exist there
Peaceful is its home
Cherished gift that remembers no wrong

Let my eyes reflect it
May my speech express it
Let my hands extend it

Precious gift, the gift of LOVE

John 13:34

If we only knew the victory won on the cross of Calvary we would not cease to rejoice.

He Reigns, and now we reign with Him.

His Victory is our Victory!

Rejoice!

Rejoice and sing the Victor's song
The battle has been won

The Lord our God is leading us
The strong and mighty One

He has fought the fight before us
Our victory secured

Praise God, our Lord, the King of Kings
The righteous loyal One

So, do not fear, do not dread
The devil a defeated foe

Rejoice! Rejoice! Our God still reigns
Now and Forevermore

1 Thessalonians 5:16

He leads me beside the still waters. There I am at peace.

We hear of wars and rumors of wars. Nightly news reports strike fear in the hearts of men. Yet, I can live in peace; in Jesus, the Prince of Peace.

I saw this bumper sticker that says it all:

No Jesus
No Peace
Know Jesus
Know Peace

Perfect Peace

Perfect peace that knows no end
Who can ever explain it
It soothes the rough waters of my life with its calm
It gives such assurance knowing I am held in His arms
I stop, I pause and think about it
This gift is from heaven
No doubt about it
It's precious and sweet
Priceless and rare
What perfect assurance
Knowing He is near
So come Holy Spirit
Fill my life with Your balm
Let me feel the protection of Your strong arm
May I share with the world the peace which I know
May I tell of God's love that they too may know

Philippians 4:6-7

One day years ago, I put my pen to the paper and this is what poured out. As I re-read it I was confused. Why did I write this? Where did it come from? What did it mean?

For over 24 years I had suffered with terrible back pain and was under constant chiropractic care. Towards the end of that time, I started experiencing hip pain and was referred for an MRI. The results came back and it was suggested that I have a hip replacement. I refused to have it and believed for a miracle of healing. At service there was often alter calls and I would go up and be prayed for believing I would be healed. At one of those alter moments the gentleman praying for me said God was showing him something. He said he saw me standing in front of a Christmas tree with a package in my hands. The package was wrapped, and that I needed to unwrap it. He told me it was a life-sized doll. He said I did not feel worthy to receive the gift, but that God wanted me to take the gift and unwrap it. God said I *was* worthy. I felt ashamed that I was refusing the gift God was offering me. I cried out to God asking for forgiveness and said I *would* receive the gift.

On my way home I was reminded of something I had written two years earlier. At home I scoured through my writings and this next poem is what I found. It was this little piece that made the puzzle pieces fit. I now understood why I wrote it years earlier. I was going to receive my healing! I wish I could say it was that simple to receive it immediately, but that was not the case. I continued to get worse and was at the point of giving up. I prayed and asked God what to do.

Finally, not seeming to get a clear answer, I relented and decided to go ahead with the surgery, since I could no longer function normally on a day-to-day basis. I believed God could heal me right up till the time of surgery. I went ahead with the surgery, and now can report I did receive my miracle! I have never had any hip pain again, but the greatest part of the miracle is that I never suffered with back pain again either. I no longer need chiropractic care, and I'm very fit and pain free. It seems God had put this story in me years before sending me a message through the prayer team member. I had not been listening.

Is God offering you a gift?
Receive your gift today!

The Christmas Gift

The day arrived, he thought it never would
Promises of gifts was what he understood
He tiptoed downstairs all expectant in wonder
Would the gifts be there?
The thought never uttered

After all he knew what he didn't care to remember
He was a bad boy right up to December
His heart skipped a beat as he took in the sight
A tree filled with presents
Could this be right?
A closer look revealed to his very surprise
A beautifully wrapped package
Tears came to his eyes
The gift tag revealed his very own name
Could it be that Santa came?
Just at that moment walking into his sight
Came his mom and his dad with looks of delight
"Open the gifts"
They said to their son
Oh no! I can't! It wouldn't be right
I've been a bad boy right up till tonight!
Hearts filled with compassion they held him real tight saying
"Son dear, we love you, that makes it alright!
The gifts are for you, it brings us great joy!
We give them with love for you are our little boy!
No! No! He responds, you do not understand!
It's not right for me to take from your hand!
A look of grief came upon their face
A crushing blow his words did make
How could it be these gifts he would refuse?
Did he not understand what he stood to lose?
How much are we like that little boy
When the gifts God gives, we too refuse?

James 1:17

Everyone needs a rock; someone to depend on during the hard times, someone stronger than ourselves.

Oftentimes it's said *religion and God are a crutch.*

I thank God I have a crutch; He is strong and stable. I am secure in Him!

The Rock

You are my Rock, O Lord!
Your foundation gives me the strength I need
Strength to keep in stable in times of uncertainty
Strength that gives me faith when
I can't see even one step in front of me
You are my Rock, O Lord
Your security gives me peace even
When my situation looks hopeless
Joy when everything looks bleak
Comfort knowing You have been faithful
In past circumstances
You are my Rock, immoveable and trustworthy
The place I run to for refuge

YOU ALONE ARE MY ROCK!

2 Samuel 22:2

Grace for the Moment

Grace for a Lifetime

Always Sufficient

Always Enough

God's

Revelation

At

Christ's

Expense

Sufficient Grace

Though darkness surrounds me
And I cannot see
His Grace is sufficient for me

The light of day fades and hope slips away
But His grace is sufficient for me

The trials they may face me
The loneliness chase me
But His grace is sufficient for me

I'll hold on to my faith and trust in His grace
For His grace is sufficient for me

2 Corinthians 12:9

The things of this world can consume us. It is so easy to lose our focus and pursue "the stuff": things that have no lasting value.

Over the last several years, I felt the need to purge myself of "stuff," so I began unloading and getting rid of things. Having recently sold my home after 29 years, I sold off some furnishings and gave away almost everything except for a few things of sentimental value. I found myself living at a friend's home, in her daughter's old room, with the remainder of my belongings in a small storage unit. I found this place to be a place of great freedom and incredible peace and joy. I have since moved to a furnished rental apartment and continue to enjoy the freedom an uncluttered life affords me.

The Gentle Hold

Hold on to nothing tightly
Release and loosen your grip
The things we have are not our own
They all belong to Him

Do not hold on with your heart
For then it just might break
These things are just a test for us
Our soul is what's at stake

Matthew 6:19-21

What greater passion can we have in life but to know the One, who, for passion, gave His life for us?

My Passion

Let the passion of my life be only for more of You Lord.

Let my eyes seek nothing other than just a glimpse of You.

Let the rhythm of my heartbeat be found in loving You.

Let the fulfillment of my dreams come from knowing You.

Psalm 27:4

Fear will paralyze us!

Fear Not! Over and over again the words of our Shepherd speak to us.

Fear and Faith cannot live together. It must be one or the other.

Where there is love, there is no fear.

Lord, help us to be fearless!

No Fear

The Lord is my Shepherd
I will not fear
Though giants surround me
I know He is near
He'll never forsake me
Never leave me alone
I'll rest in His presence
And trust in His care
Don't be discouraged
Don't let joy slip away
The Savior is near you
He is leading the way

1 John 4:18

Sometimes we grow weary. The way grows hard. Trials come. They press in and try to suffocate us.

But, victory is ahead. He has already won the battle.

He has provided your armor and everything else you need to assure the Victory!

Never Give Up!
No, Never!

Press On

Press on through the battles
Be courageous and bold
Hold on to the promise
Streets paved with gold
Find strength for the journey
In the joy that He gives
Just fight the good fight
His Word is your shield

Put on your armor
Press on don't retreat
The sword of the Spirit
Everyday read
He'll never forsake you
Never leave you alone
Press on in the battle
He'll meet every need

Ephesians 6:11-18

There is a joyful song coming from those who have been redeemed. Who else can sing with such fervent affection, such tremendous joy, such uninhibited passion as one who has been in bondage without hope and then been released from a hellish place!

Redeemed

Redeemed
I've been bought with a price
Redeemed
Paid for by His sacrifice

No longer a prisoner
My chains now are gone
My debt has been cancelled
Atonement is mine

I'll live in the freedom this purchase has gained
I'll bask in His goodness
I'll sing out His praise

Redeemed! Redeemed!
My soul has been redeemed!

Revelations 5:9

Too often we forget to give thanks. Out of ten lepers whom Jesus healed, only *one* took the time to stop and say thank you. How often do we forget what we were saved from?

Lord, help us to remember!

I Remember

I remember the struggle
But now I've been set free
The pain
But now I am totally healed
I remember the sorrow
But now I have been made glad
The confusion
But now I am at peace
I remember the emptiness
But now I am satisfied
The turmoil
But now I am safe
I remember the hopelessness
But now the future is bright
I remember how I was lost
But now I have been found
I remember my sin
But now I have a Savior
I remember my past
But now I have an eternity promised
I remember the cross
And what it cost

I Remember
I WILL NEVER FORGET!

Psalm 77:11

We are in the grip of His grace.

His hands are big enough to create the galaxies, yet gentle enough to hold us in the palm of His hand.

Knowing (trusting) His grip, we can let go and let God.

The Grip

The grip of God's hand upon my life
Is what gives me the strength to go on
Should He let me go I'd surely fall
For I have no strength of my own
His hold is gentle
Loving and strong
Leading me on life's way
In His grip I'll stay the rest of my days
Trusting He'll lead the way

Psalm 139:10

Being involved in evangelism enlarges one's perspective on God's love for the lost. Stepping out of our comfort zone is not easy.

Why do we have to be so concerned about the lost anyway?
Someone else will witness to them.
They don't want to hear it anyway.
They don't want to have religion *shoved* down their throats.

We have so many reasons, so many excuses. We may not all be evangelists, but if only we could move past our comfort zone and share with that *one* lost sheep the Lord has put in our path.

We can make a difference!

Beyond Our Comfort Zone

Comfort!
Even the word itself can make us feel snug and secure.
It leaves us feeling peaceful and undisturbed.
Oh! How we love the feeling.
But what is at stake?
What is the cost?

Do we not see that the enemy of our souls
Is using this distraction to lull us to sleep?
How unreliable are our feelings!
Multitudes being lost for eternity while we sleep!

Who of us seeing a person who is blind and deaf
Walking into traffic would not run ahead into the
Traffic to spare the life of one about to lose it?

Why then are we who have spiritual eyes and ears
Not running out into the world to save those who do not
Hear and do not see from an eternity in hell?

Let us remember that when Christ hung on the cross
He was not comfortable!
He left a heavenly throne and gave up the comforts of
Heaven to take up the uncomfortable position on the cross.
He was moved with compassion past his fleshly desires
Seeing with an eternal perspective what was at stake.

So, dear God, as we are to be growing in our likeness of Christ
Let us also give up our fleshly desires and comforts and
Have that same eternal perspective.

Help us Lord to move out of our "Comfort Zones"

Mark 16:15

Everyone loves to receive gifts. We remember those treasured gifts long after they are gone. We remember the feelings they brought and the love we felt by the giver.

We can also choose not to receive a gift. How sad!

Healing is a gift...Receive it!

The Gift

There is a gift of greatest price
Purchased long ago
The gift of healing by His stripes
I heard that this was so

How was it that I did not have
This gift whose price was paid
Could it be I did not believe
His blood had set me free

The truth now known I will be bold
And take hold of what is mine
I come to Christ the crucified
And receive my gift divine

1 Peter 2:24

When we are unfaithful, He is faithful still.

Amazing, Agape Love!

Faithful

Faithful Lord oh let me be
Faithful Lord to only Thee

I give my life to You alone
All that I have to You I owe

You've proved Yourself in many ways
You've been with me through all my days

The times I failed
You stayed true
Awaiting my return to You

This faithfulness I could not earn
A love so true please let me learn

1 Thessalonians 5:24

LOVE NEVER FAILS

Fully Loved

Fully and completely loved
What a state of bliss
No other feeling can compare
With knowing I am His

Soaking in His presence
I set my gaze on Him
All I see is His sweet face
Looking down on me

Now all the cares of this life
Melt and fade away
No other love do I need
Completely I am His

John 13:1

How can we know the victory if there is no battle?

How can we overcome if there is nothing in our way?

How can we learn patience if there is nothing to test us?

The Road to Victory

The trials of life He'll not remove
The obstacles we'll need
How can we prove we'll overcome
If there's nothing to impede

The Spirit is our teacher
The lessons are hard to learn
He teaches in the school of life
Our welfare His concern

He teaches there is victory
Though through the trials we must go
He teaches us to overcome
And how this must be done

It must be done with patience
Perseverance is the key
We'll never know if we give up
The way to victory

1 Corinthians 15:57

Many of us have suffered the pain of a broken heart, broken relationships, broken dreams and broken promises.

Shattered Hearts

The good news is there is no heart too hard, no heart beyond repair in the loving hands of Jesus.

He can make all things new.

The Calloused Heart

The calloused heart once sweet and pure
Once filled with hope and joy
Now in a grave caused by bitter pain
No hope of life remains

How did it come to be so hard
Unfeeling and refrained
A slow and steady sure retreat
From those who watch in vain

The cry for help it did not come
Alone you came to be
Withdrawn aloof no tenderness
Afraid of all you see

Oh calloused heart death need not be
Hope is still alive
Just reach out to the Savior's hand
His healing touch supplied

It will heal the wounded places
He'll melt the heart of stone
He'll restore in you a brand new heart
And make it all His own

What can you lose?
A calloused Heart
Which is of no use you see
Trade it for a brand new heart
Soft and new and clean

Isaiah 61:1

Sometimes we mess up in life:

Bad choices
Wrong turns
Faulty navigating devices

We cannot change the past, but we can take a new direction and change our future. Have you found yourself in a ditch?

Today is a new day!

Hope

Hope…What is this illusive thing?
I see it in the distance
I long for it but cannot seem to obtain it
I come closer to it but as I reach for it
Like a mist it dissolves between my fingers
Oh how my soul yearns for this thing

Is it real…Does it exist?
Hope, why have I not found you?
Where do you hide?
Like a mirage you disappear as I come closer

Hope…Where have you gone?
Where do I find you
God allow me to see
Grant me discernment
My questions need answers

How do I go on without hope?
I fall to my knees
I call out to you God
My questions are silenced in the stillness of Your presence
I feel your peace
Hope must be nearby
I reach out…Can I touch it?
Like the heat from the sun it cannot be touched
But I can feel its warmth

Reality lightens the way
Hope is there
Another day…another chance…a new beginning…HOPE

Proverbs 13:12

The Potter's Hand: Gentle Yet Strong

The Lump of Clay: Moldable

The Finished Product: A Masterpiece!

94

The Process

The process is painful yet well underway
When once we surrender to His will and His ways
He has a great purpose of this I am sure
He wants to refine us to be pure as gold
The process is lengthy
No shortcuts to take
Gently He'll mold us
We'll otherwise break

So come Holy Spirit
Your will my desire
Come take my hand and bring me up higher
Higher to where only few dare to tread
Casting out demons and raising the dead
Display your great power through me everyday
My vessel I empty
Now fill it I pray

The process ongoing
There's work to be done
Don't stop the process till I look like Your SON!

Jeremiah 18:4

The resurrection of Christ gives us hope and a chance for new beginnings. When we are in a tomb of sin we desperately need someone to roll the stone away and un-wrap our grave clothes. This is what our Savior did for us. It is our decision whether we will remain in the tomb or step out into the Dawn.

Dawn of a New Day

Let the dawn break out in all her glory
May her light burst forth in splendor
A New Day has begun and it is glorious!
There is hope for a new beginning like the freshness of spring

The frost of winter now turns to warmth
Melted snow is but a faded memory
The gusty winds die down and are now but a soft cool breeze
Bitter cold relents and the noonday sun takes a bow
The dreariness of winter is over, fading away like the night
Anticipation of joyful days, fill the heart with a song
Death is overshadowed by resurrection power

Dawn begins a new day
There is hope for healing, making all things new
Forgiveness restoring what was stolen from you
There is love to cover a multitude of sins
Joy to give strength that comes from within
Peace and contentment now brighten the day

The night is over, it's the Dawn of a New Day!

2 Peter 1:19

In this life we will surely experience tribulation; Jesus did. Is a servant greater than his master? But for the joy set before Him, Jesus endured the cross. He now sits at the right hand of the Father.

Keep on weary one.
Live with an eternal perspective!

The Best is Yet to Come

The caterpillar has struggled; now the butterfly has its glorious wings unwrapped.

The branch has fought through the winter's snow, but spring has sent forth its bud; now the rose is in full bloom.

The storm clouds have poured down their rain; but now the most beautiful rainbow has appeared in its entire splendor.

The farmer labors, the work is daunting; a bountiful harvest now his reward.

The surrendered life a struggle; victory promised.

Nature sings her song; be sure, **the best is yet to come!**

2 Corinthians 4:17

Ending Notes and Prayer

Special thanks to all my readers. I hope and pray that these poems have encouraged you and brought hope and a greater revelation of the riches that we have in Jesus Christ.

To my readers who may not have placed their faith in Christ Jesus, this book would be incomplete without me sharing the Good News of salvation. You can come to know Him and have the free gift of eternal life. You can do so by acknowledging that your sin has separated you from God. The Ten Commandments reveal what sin is, and if we are honest with ourselves we will admit that we have not kept God's laws. Then in a spirit of repentance, truly confess your sins before God and acknowledge your need for a savior. Invite Christ Jesus to be Lord and Savior of your life. Receive this gift by faith. I invite you to do so today.

It is the greatest decision you will ever make.

In His Love,
Alba

Acknowledgements:

First and foremost to my Heavenly Father, all glory belongs to You alone! I pray that this book will point others to Jesus Christ who alone is the way to the Father. In You are the answers to all life's questions. I could not have done this without the guidance of Your Holy Spirit. I am forever Yours!

Many thanks, to Krista, Deborah and the entire team at Creative Force Press Publishing. Krista and Deborah thank you for pushing me past what I thought was my limit! I could not have done this without you!

To my special friend Vickie Moller, thank you for all your encouragement. You gave me courage to overcome my insecurities. You are an inspiration! Thank you also for referring me to CFP.

Additional thanks to Pastor Cam and Nancy Colombo, Al and Judy Castaldo, Jennifer Esposito, Cara and Greg Smyth, and Becky and Pete Ferraro for all your love, prayers and support over the years.

About the Author:

Alba McCarthy was born and raised in Brooklyn, New York, and now resides in Long Island. She is the seventh child of 17 children. Alba is the mother of three wonderful children; James, Stephen and Crystal. She is also the grandmother of two of the most amazing little girls, Chloe Rae and Mackenzie Rose.

To Contact Alba: <u>albam122@yahoo.com</u>

Notes and Thoughts:

Notes and Thoughts:

Notes and Thoughts:

Notes and Thoughts:

Notes and Thoughts:

Dawn of a New Day is proudly published by:

Creative Force Press
Guiding Aspiring Authors to Release Their Dream

www.CreativeForcePress.com

Do You Have a Book in You?

Made in the USA
Charleston, SC
27 June 2014